When You Ask Me, "Why Paris?"

poems by

Michelle Ortega

Finishing Line Press
Georgetown, Kentucky

When You Ask Me,
"Why Paris?"

ACKNOWLEDGMENTS

I am grateful to the following publications for including these pieces, or versions of:

Platform Review: "After and Before," "The Shape of Someday," "Thirty-Third Murder"
Rust + Moth: "Revival at the Hôtel Biron"
Exit 13: "Show Me," "Love Lock," "On the Pont Alexander III"
Contemporary Haibun Online, How to Write a Form Poem (TS Poetry Press): "Let the Questions Go Unanswered"
Stillwater Review: "la danse," "arrival"
Snapdragon, Journal of Healing: "Eggshell"
Look Up, Arts by the People: "A Study in Water"
Don't Ask Why: "Van Gogh's Room at L'Auberge Ravoux," "Show Me," "Let the Questions go Unanswered," "Eggshell" "Monday Morning Orbit" "Thirty-Third Murder" and "Unshielded"

Publisher: Leah Huete de Maines
Editor: Christen Kincaid
Cover Art: Michelle Ortega
Author Photo: Paul Rabinowitz
Cover Design: Anna Hershinow

Order online: www.finishinglinepress.com
also available on amazon.com

Author inquiries and mail orders:
Finishing Line Press
PO Box 1626
Georgetown, Kentucky 40324
USA

Contents

For all who wander
and find themselves at home
on every journey

After and Before

New Year's Eve, 1993

was an ending, although I didn't recognize it then; I numbed myself for that world-halting kiss at the altar, didn't know I could walk away, or run; I forgot about Paris, but remembered to move carefully in raw silk—the gown, delicate, no pockets—and to sneak outside and smoke a Marlboro light with my cousin's wife, and to watch fireworks over the field at midnight; I remember dancing with my bridesmaids, no groom in sight, all the champagne toasts and me, sober, realizing I had no voice as I mouthed "I do," because I didn't; I remember the photographer was so efficient, each photo so carefully posed, ordinary, airbrushed later for perfection; after the divorce, I bundled the album for trash, satisfied when it hit the bottom of the can.

New Year's Eve, 1989

was a beginning, although I didn't recognize it then; I ached for a world-altering kiss at midnight, but the one I received was dry and common; I forgot about the boy, but still remember the softness of my Levi button-fly's after a week of travel, and the way a matchbook slid under my palm from the back pocket, and the Gauloises in my bag, and the Eiffel Tower backlit with fireworks at midnight; I remember a bottle of wine passed between friends, winding through crowds on les grands boulevards, shouting *bonne année á tout le monde!* until I was hoarse; I remember that night in black and white, fuzzy focus because I shot film with my Minolta x700; I still feel the camera in my hand, its coolness pressed to my cheek, the shutter's pulse with each exposure.

The Shape of Someday

On the family room floor,
my daughter and I lay flat
in front of a box fan,
and stave off the first heat
blast of summer vacation.
Lately we speak the language
of careful words (mine)
and death stares (hers)
and slammed doors (ours),
but a movie and morning
inertia nudge us together
with little energy for more.
I have to thank Remy, that
gourmet-cooking, looking-
for-his-place-in-the-world
rat from *Ratatouille*—
misunderstood by his family,
separated from the colony,
he emerges from a terror-tour
of the sewers onto Parisian
streets. As he marvels at
the animated Eiffel Tower,
my rising eighth-grader lets
her wish loose: *someday, I
want to go to Paris.* I made
the same wish in eighth
grade; to her, too quickly,
I reply: *someday,* we will.
For the rest of that week,
I can't swallow the shape
of *someday* on my tongue.

arrival

a long flight later
I know the ocean
won't part   ready
to restart   lucid eyes
daughter beside me
far from the place
I exist (if not live)
I remember little

about this city
about my body
before   but I know
I am my own country
unknown territory
I am a map-maker
not running away
from something

running back to me

shadowSelf

I.

I don't feel   anything
she feels everything   lurks
just below my surface

shatters glass

from the fragments Picasso-me
looks up   crooked smiles
when a sharp edge

bleeds my finger

II.

I wear a black hoodie
to sleep   but
she finds me
reminds me

I want to be like the tree
who forgets the storm
     each lost leaf
before winter sleep

she keeps the memories

triggers the cough
when I speak

that was now
this is then

I want to be held
don't touch me

III.

I fear her   fear being her
   although she has no body
                she is drowning

Revival at the Hôtel Biron
Musée Rodin, Paris

I had never known the passion
Rodin lifted from stone into light—

contours like silk embrace, whisper
in shadows; kneel flesh before flesh,

holy; gather energy between palms,
a universe. I wander room after room

until I find *The Hand of God* on
a wooden pedestal, close enough

to touch; I turn the piece slowly, see
the sinews, knuckles and fingernails

of the Master hand, and his children,
still part of the earth, not fully formed,

but held—I lay under his chisel as
He lifts me from stone into light.

A Coke and a Café au Lait

Elbow-to-elbow with locals, we sit outside no matter the weather. In the Eighteenth there are fewer tourists, less high fashion. More strollers and dogs and kids on their way home from school. A man with a baguette under the arm. A woman on her phone, sturdy-stepped in the highest heels. The grocer across the street, deftly wrapping fruit in parchment paper.

Our order, always the same: hers, *du Coca et des escargots*, mine, *un café au lait*. I prefer deep-heated caffeine and frothy milk, but I ask my daughter for a sip of her Coke, from the bottle. I've long given up the drink but its sweetness, here, is pleasing. When our food arrives, my daughter offers me an escargot—I decline (it's a texture thing), but reach across the table and dip some baguette in the garlic and parsley butter on the dish.

Escort

Where Monet and his family are buried
in Giverny, even the cats are unseen—
turned ghost, turned particle, earthly
business finished, left for weather
and soil to reclaim. Ribboned grey
over grey, the sky; horizon, marigold
and umber. Perfectly October, contrast
from the day before, when my daughter
and I walk to the Montmartre cemetery
from our hotel; noontime sun blazes,
creates strobes, sharp shadows; traffic
noise from every angle jumps the stone
perimeter; burial in progress (we don't
want to disturb), so we turn to another
lane, empty— except for a black cat
who escorts us down the cobbled path,
weaves around chapels, headstones,
our legs, prevents us from lingering.
Too much going on, perhaps confusion
for the newly arrived, newly departed;
we turn to thank our guide as we go,
but he has already disappeared.

Picnic

I've only eaten figs
at Thanksgiving, dried,

so I have no idea
how delicate the skin,

how unexpected when
I lift a purple jewel

with greedy, careless
fingers   and it splits,

exposing the magenta
false-flesh, tiny blooms—

nectar drips through
my fingers before

I inhale the first,
the sweetest bite.

Undo This Doing

That scowl, just for me—every time I turn the camera toward her. She thinks I'll forgo the shot, but it's her first time in Paris, our first time here together. No way I'm letting go. I see the sun-freckles on her scrunched nose, and the way the light hits her bangs, dyed pink, and her thick waves, curled like the ocean's edge. The angle of her chin—it juts out, just a little when she's quiet, and even more when she defies what's going on around her. I wish I had scowled more when I was young. My daughter thinks she can scare me away, that I'll give up, but I won't—I zoom in closer, closer, and by the third shot she looks right at me and we crack up.

Eggshell

The remnant, a smooth blue vessel in the sun. A universe expands; the hatchling, translucent, breaks through with delicate bones, imagines feathers and flight.

Anything can be a trigger—a tight collar, the morning news, a waft of Marlboro reds over coffee. Half a robin's eggshell, weightless on the grass, blown far from the nest that held it. I am at once, here, walking to my car, and there, on the ground beside a pond. Here, it is daytime. I have errands to run before work. There, it is night and I am pressed to the earth.

Love Lock

One summer Saturday, I walk
West Houston, toward SoHo;
moving slow, the weight of my camera
in hand soothes me, persuades me
to press on in heat so thick, even
the tall-building shades overhead
doesn't relieve it; about half
a block away, a single padlock
hangs on a chain-link fence,

reminds me of a bridge in Paris,
locks hung by lovers in eternal vow;
off the Seine, November rawness
gusts through my hair—I yearn
for some promise of my own;
that was before so many locks
become an eyesore, their collective
weight too much for the railings,
before I knew I held my own key;

as I approach the lone padlock,
here, grateful for solitude and
a morning to wander the city,
I see her: a girl, the photo taped
where lovers' initials are carved;
her eyes—an indigo ocean,
deep, where the current is slow
and strong and shapes the earth,
unseen; *never truly alone*, she tells me.

muse

across
the courtyard

a woman smokes
in the winter air

without
a shiver

la danse

a winter
breath
slips
through
the window
bumps
my coffee's
steam
into
a drowsy
pirouette

shift

...and then one day,
morning light decorates
the hardwood floor
and the bare walls
and that one spot
on the kitchen counter,
and you catch refraction
and lace and stretchy
shadows all around you;
maybe it's from the book
you picked up at the airport
shop, maybe a song you
haven't heard in years runs
on repeat in your head; maybe
therapy is working after all—
probably all these things
combined but suddenly you
breathe like you used to,
like you deserve to, and you
remember something from
your life before; it carves
another line on the map you
follow; it's a river rushing,
rushing away from its source
not to escape, but to expand
and you remember something
that makes you smile,
that makes you gasp in wonder
at who you were, and a little
sad you couldn't see it then;
maybe it's the note left
in a cubby in a hallowed
bookstore in a gothic city
that helps you realize we are
all on a journey, not the same

and the same journey, both,
and without thinking,
in the present and the past
you linger all at once.

Tu Me Manques

Perhaps the sound
of pen scratching
over creamy paper,
just one true sentence
can be enough,
but my own truth
eludes me after
so much energy spent
not remembering—
which is different
than forgetting. I leave
the Moleskine empty,
leave the cozy
apartment and walk,
instead, through the 18th,
search for a story
that is not my own,
that is shiny surface
and distracting.
Every secondhand
line falls flat until
somewhere along
the cobbled Rue Lepic,
I step on a curb
to avoid ghostly hoof
and wagon wheel,
and I am stunned,
realize how often
I move aside to avoid
things that no longer
exist. Memories trickle
in, and when, once
again, the blank page
invites me, dares me
to begin I admit:

I miss you. I say this
to myself—I miss the way
I used to feel, to speak
without filter or fear.
The French phrase it
like this: *tu me manques.*
You are missing
from me   I write.

Monday Morning Orbit
Montmartre, France

At home, laundry happens between paying bills, meal prep, Saturday morning clean up. Sometimes the last load rests in the dryer, long-cold, until I need clean pants or my favorite socks. The machines are small, tucked away in a closet.

In Paris, little worlds spin around me. Coffee from a French press—the grounds, the spoon, the plunge. Spokes of a bike wheel, shadow long on the street. At the bottom of the hill, a carousel: gaudy horses, a golden woman with blank eyes, captive on the center drum. A dragon in flight.

At *la laverie*, garments float and tumble, my reflection steady on the plexiglass door. A man tosses wet sheets into an empty dryer; I catch his eye as he turns to leave. Outside the window, he lights a cigarette, flicks ash on the sidewalk.

Let the Questions Go Unanswered

A Sphinx with a warrior's breastplate and headdress guards the garden. It's 82° in October; I have no wisdom for her riddle, but she allows my daughter and I to pass through.

Vines climb nearby buildings, remind us of a cemetery in Paris. Roses strain toward the sun, bees fervent over echinacea, tiny pineapples sprout in metal urns. An iguana with a turquoise collar sun on the back of a stone lion, its thin leash drops to the owner on a bench below.

Old bookstore scents blend with turning leaves and overripe butterfly bushes. A Grecian woman rises amid the SoHo backdrop.

> delicate concrete
> one bare breast—
> her dress pressed by a breeze

Van Gogh's Room at L'Auberge Ravoux
Auvers-Sur-Oise, France

Outside the inn, wave on wave of color: cloud and sky and wheat and bloom. More than impressions, he painted *alive*, he painted *trembling*. He painted the hum of the stars' origin song.

Inside his room, we semi-circle the tour guide, but I hardly hear what she says. I look to the skylight, to the single chair beneath it. A stir, wordless, swells around me—palm up, I reach for the intangible: the hand that held the brush, that held the gun.

Self-Portrait, Vincent
Musée D'Orsay, Paris

alive—
the brush stroke's
weight and wave

beyond sharp angles
and shadow,
painted vibration

blue eyes pierce,
        glass shatters

forbidden,
I press my lips
to his

Thirty-Third Murder

We glide down the Seine on a tourist boat, past the charred Notre Dame and her barricaded Île de la Cité, past the walkway near the river below, where weeds push through cracks, collect windblown litter, where graffiti on the high wall catches my eye: a poster, not one poster but one hand-painted letter per poster DOLORES A ÉTÉ ETRANGLÉE ICI PAR SON MARI; I don't snap a shot, although I have a cloud full of street art from all the places we've strolled, as if the memorial would be defiled by curiosity, and then I wonder how much more defiled *Dolores* can be, and remember how the jeweler wouldn't price my engagement ring when I tried to sell it (he didn't want to insult me) and I told him there couldn't be anything worse than what I already suffered (he gave me two hundred for it); I wonder, can I say *strangled* if I survived, if someday I can stop speaking about what happened, or should I never stop because *Dolores, 40 Ans, 33ième morte,* can't ever speak again, all the while the sun—the sun—pinks my face gently.

Notre Dame, Burning

It's one of those Mondays. I'm two weeks behind before I open the door to my office. Paperwork due, emailing awaiting reply—all pressing a schedule with back-to-back patients. A group chat with my daughter and her dad can't wait—she's not finishing her thesis in time to graduate—but has to; in the background, my mind spins a response for hours.

Friends text me with footage of the bad news. Spires alight, roof aflame; Notre Dame is burning. Crowds overwhelm the streets, lift psalm and prayer that merge with thick black plume, but also block the fire brigade. I'm not sure how much more I can absorb, I've already put out so many fires today. This one, in every way, out of my reach. I want to cry, but there's no space for that right now. I take a deep breath and remember her strength, make it my own: *Notre Dame has burned before, and she will recover this time, too.*

Show Me
Père Lachaise Cemetery, Paris, France

I first spot the rough black letters painted on the tree—*Can you show me the way to the next whiskey bar*—and almost overlook the plain headstone for James Douglas Morrison, his gravesite adorned with cigarette butts and an empty beer can. The epitaph, in ancient Greek, translates: *True to his spirit.* Or, perhaps, *True to his demon.*

When I was 14, I pinned all *The Doors* album covers to my bedroom wall, spun the thick vinyl on a cheap record player. I dreamt of a pilgrimage to Père Lachaise, and of Jim's return (his death a hoax); I've finally arrived. I think about all the "Jims" I've loved since then, what they have taken, what they have left. Now, I stand here with my daughter, and I wonder what cords will hold fast, will keep her feet moving, will weave through us both. *No one here gets out alive,* Jim said. I am here, still alive, and as we head back to the metro I sing to myself: *Oh, don't ask why, oh, don't ask why.*

Unshielded
Jardin de Luxembourg, Paris

Many mothers hover
over their children
in the park, but one
young girl plays alone.
She carries her boat
with outstretched arms,
leans back a bit,
balances her little frame.
It's early summer, mild;
I watch as she plunks
the boat into the water,
sets a course and, tall
pole in hand, gives it
a shove. The sail catches
a steady breeze and they're
off! With the pole high
in one hand, she runs
around the fountain,
eyes fixed on her vessel.
Unshielded, she conquers.

I'm Drunk!

"On wine, poetry or virtue, as you wish. But be drunk."
    —Beaudelaire

I'm drunk
with early morning
room sways
sleep-waking spins

I'm cobblestone-
cobbling
red wine chortling
while pieces
of dreams
flash and float away

try to remember
where I was
last night
last year
last life

but only
this moment
matters

drunk on the rush
of being
drunk on the rush
of love
after all this time
I love
my life

On the Pont Alexandre III
Paris, France

Just before midnight
a storm passes,
washes Paris clean
of daytime fervor—
I wander toward
the bridge, which
is often four-deep
in tourists, now nearly
empty except for myself,
some couples and a few
solitary *flâneurs*.

The gilt Fames on each
corner tower over nymphs
and cherubs nestled
between art deco lamps.
Lights from the next bridge
over bejewel the Seine
like Van Gogh's *Starry Night
over the Rhône*, the energy
of each brushstroke
on the water.

I imagine my daughter
beside me, but she
is elsewhere. Stars
above the clouds
backlight inky sky,
jasmine amplifies
the damp night air.
When the Iron Lady
sparkles at midnight
I am held in quiet magic,
open to her invitation.

A Study in Water
after Monet

Night

Moonless night, not moonless the sky
but moon-hidden, the moon inside
me; beside this obsidian pond I sit,
slip my naked body, like quill into well
through the surface; the water the air
I sink under and float above, swallow
night-ink, swallow shadows that hover,
that cover my hunger, from darkness
I whisper through the darkness, search
for what exists, what has been forgotten,
has forgotten, search for words, stirred
only to find them close, so close, as if the
hidden moon scrolled them across my skin.

Morning

Unhurried, morning embraces me
as the waterlily rises from dark soil
to light, as she rests on the surface
between water and air, as her petals
open toward citrine mist; I, too,
surface-dwell, open—my slow breath
undulates still waters, create a tide
that bounces off the pond's edges,
returns to me; in the hush of mind,
tranquility, in tranquility, no bounds
between inner and outer energies;
I am fully present, fully connected
to ancient memory, future possibility.

Afternoon

This shallow body reflects infinity,
reflects no-ceiling height behind
gauzy periwinkle, and at the edge
of this shallow body, my body; I
am a silhouette at the grassy bank
undisturbed, undisturbing until
I lean in and graze treetop, reach for
a cloud expecting sticky, expecting
sweetness only to find a breech
in this liminal space; this shallow
body reflects inversion, where above
is below; I am a ripple disturbing cool
glass; in quiet chaos, I ripple the sky.

In Appreciation

The writing life is often a solitary one, but I give thanks for the following mentors and fellow poets, whom I also know as friends:

The Westfield Poetry Group led by Adele Kenny, with Nancy Lubarsky, Bob Rosenbloom, Tom Plante and Basil Rassoukus for great stories, laughter and honest poetry work around the dining room table; Dimitri Reyes, whose joyful, loving energy gathers an amazing online workshop community; Daniel Welch, my poetry-soul friend; Jacinta White, who challenged me to know my own voice more deeply; Charlotte Donlon and the Spiritual Direction for Writers™ co-writing community to make the writing process more consistent and less lonely; Paul Rabinowitz and ARTS by the People for friendship, guidance and meaningful arts opportunities; Laura Barkat and Tweetspeak Poetry community for being there "from the beginning."

You've all enriched my journey in unspeakable ways; I am the writer I am today because of you.

To my daughter, Tori: Thank you for making this journey with me, for reading drafts and believing in my work whole-heartedly. It's truly the greatest gift to be your mom. I love you.

Michelle Ortega is a speech-language pathologist and founder of her private practice, Communicare Ltd., Inc., where she uses holistic practices to support communication development and recovery. She is the author of *Don't Ask Why* (limited edition chapbook, Seven Kitchens Press) and *Tissue Memory* (microchapbook, Porkbelly Press).

Michelle's writing has also been published at *Tweetspeak Poetry, Tiferet Journal, Exit 13, Snapdragon: A Journal of Healing, Platform Review, Shot Glass Journal, Paterson Literary Review, Rust + Moth, Humana Obscura, Stillwater Review* and elsewhere, online and in print.

She was selected as the 2023-24 "Poet Laura" of Tweetspeak Poetry where she wrote monthly columns on the exploration and joy of integrating poetry into daily life.

Michelle was selected to participate in the Writing Lab Ekphrastic Summer Residency through ARTS by the People (2023), and is published in its collaborative journal *Look Up!* Other anthologies and collections include Earthsong by TS Poetry Press, *How to Write a Form Poem* by TS Poetry Press, *Casual* (e-book) by TS Poetry Press, *New Jersey Bards Poetry Review 2023 & 2024*, and most recently, *I Tried Not To Write*, by SnapDragon, a Journal of Art and Healing.

She currently serves on the Board of Directors at ARTS by the People, and led the Writing Lab Ekphrastic Summer residency (2024), as well as co-edited the collaborative journal, *Like Waves Through Flesh*.

For more about Michelle, please visit her website at *www.michelleortegawrites.com*